T0166484

LETTERS TO BORGES

BOOKS BY STEPHEN KUUSISTO

Poetry

Letters to Borges
Only Bread, Only Light

Memoir

Eavesdropping: A Memoir of Blindness and Listening
Planet of the Blind

Nonfiction

Do Not Interrupt: A Playful Take on the Art of Conversation
The Poet's Notebook (editor, with Deborah Tall and David Weiss)

STEPHEN KUUSISTO

LETTERS TO BORGES

Copper Canyon Press
Port Townsend, Washington

Copyright 2013 by Stephen Kuusisto

Printed in the United States of America

Cover art: Rosamond Purcell, *Malmaison II*

Copper Canyon Press is in residence at Fort Worden State Park in Port Townsend, Washington, under the auspices of Centrum. Centrum is a gathering place for artists and creative thinkers from around the world, students of all ages and backgrounds, and audiences seeking extraordinary cultural enrichment.

LIBRARY OF CONGRESS CATALOGING-IN-PUBLICATION DATA
Kuusisto, Stephen.
Letters to Borges / Stephen Kuusisto.
  p. cm.
ISBN 978-1-55659-386-4 (alk. paper)
I. Title.
PS3561.U85L48 2012
811′.54—dc23

2012029078

9 8 7 6 5 4 3 2 FIRST PRINTING

Copper Canyon Press
Post Office Box 271
Port Townsend, Washington 98368

www.coppercanyonpress.org

For Connie

ACKNOWLEDGMENTS

Grateful acknowledgment is made to the editors of publications in which the following poems, some in earlier versions, first appeared:

The Bark: "Elegy for a Guide Dog"

Beloit Poetry Journal: "Jazz from Cripple City"

The Iowa Review: "The Lottery Sellers," "Prose Poem Written at 2 a.m."

MiPOesias: "By Halves," "The War Production Canzone"

Ragged Edge: "Elegy for Lucy Grealy," "Elegy for Ray Charles and His Mother," "Kansas: Deaf Girl Watching the Moon"

Red Wheelbarrow: "Borges: They Are Knocking the Wind out of Me in Iowa City," "Letter to Borges from Porvoo, Finland," "Letter to Borges from Tampere, Finland"

Sweet: "Autobiographia Literaria"

This Art: Poems about Poetry: "Erasing Stars," "They Say"

And soon, in the coming nights,
we will appear, like wandering actors,
each in the other's dream
and in the dreams of strangers whom we didn't know together.

YEHUDA AMICHAI (TRANSLATED BY
CHANA BLOCH AND STEPHEN MITCHELL)

CONTENTS

1

2

4

LETTERS TO BORGES

1

Now is it a tree or a god there, showing through the rusted gate?

JORGE LUIS BORGES
(TRANSLATED BY W.S. MERWIN)

Emily Dickinson and the Ophthalmoscope

1

A bird, dun-colored and nearly bald, flits above the retina and vanishes
        Like a Calvinist toy—a straw doll lost in snow.
"I am a girl going blind," she thinks. "Soon I will be dark as a hat
Or something we might lace."

        Of talk there is no use—
The tongue itself is blanked,
One might speak to sleeves
Or the buttons of Father's shirt.
        Still the bird returns
And walks across the eye
Like Milton's Eve, dream-walking.
        "To think what I may tell it," she thinks. "That's the trick—
A small blind wisdom as winter ends."
        She sees the bird already knows:
It bathes itself,
Then tucks to clean its wings.
        My cocoon tightens, colors tease,
        I am feeling for the air;
        A dim capacity for wings.

2

To be blind is the end of autumn.
Watch as the afternoon falls like seeds;
Keep a locket; press the sights.

5

The Sun kept setting—setting—still
No Hue of Afternoon—
Upon the Village I perceived—
From House to House 'twas Noon—

The Dusk kept dropping—dropping—still
No Dew upon the Grass—
But only on my Forehead stopped—
And wandered in my Face—

What medicine for this?
Earthen face and clay eyes.

3

I see the doctor's skill
Is made of repetition;
Lens after lens he tries;
But strangest
Is a difference.

He sees the planet rise
In the blank sky of faith,
My eye,
Too blind, he says, for day
But equal to twilight.

He looks long
Where nothing moves

But inscape blood
Those hairs of anemone,
Garnet script,
Mine alone.

I won't go blind,
He says,
Though much will be gained
Or lost
By thinking so.

Home again at nightfall;
The cemetery grass
Fills with fireflies —
And as he promised
I alone see
How, giddy with parturition,
They circle
Amid the graves.

Write It Down

for James Crenner

The last crickets sing
Of synesthesia:
Leg on leg,
Their wings
Cold as glass.
My dear friend Sisi
From Finland
Tells me
The crickets
Prepare winter music.
Half sad, half
Clinging to heat.
We laugh
In her garden
Thinking of crickets
As Lutherans
In a sacristy.

How could a song of legs
Equal belief?
We know and don't know.
Walking in the tall grass
The Finns call "horse weed"—
Shaggy, rough, purple,
And bruised as twilight—
We hear crickets on all sides
And my friend says:
"Crickets don't know if sunlight

Is ever coming back,
That is what we call
The name of the tune."

The Books to Come

Better than the view of Mississippi clouds
Floating like mares' tails
But not better than our own sky,
The books to come.

This morning, wherever
We open our hands,
We are alive like animals:
Truthful, making our way,
Nerves and muscles strict,
Green maps in our minds.

Ahead of us the day waves long branches
And the grass offers resolution
And the solarium of each minute
Draws us into chances,
And every embrace of time

Tricks us into myth.
Better than the view from fields
The books to come,
Better than the natural melody of rain
The books to come. Likely

To save us
Like secret friends, books to come
Like hopes and intervals of hope,
Books out there
To be read in the hush of days.

The ripening of fruit in the books to come;
The names of imagined children;
The "go ahead"; the "as always";
The "necessary"; the "needing to cross";
Not better than your life but the life you will know.

Letter to Borges from Buenos Aires

Things seen
Through the eyes of girls —
Morning walks
Past intricate, modernist shopping,
A touch of Milan in the old city —
Glass flutes, gold medallions,
Baskets filled with carved birds.

Borges, tell them what *you* see:
Wingless angels, brows unselfish,
Books blown open
From which numbers rise and walk
Like circus cats.

Today's girl describes carpets and last year's wine,
You clutch her arm, afraid to walk.
Such stark houses, iron grilles,
Perforated clocks —
All things
Confessing station
To the blind.

Is this why you stayed home,
Behind a window, water in a glass,
Leaves and shutters "imperative," "irrevocable"?

Letter to Borges in His Parlor

What will become of you
With your Anglican heart and old furniture?
Are you waiting for insects at the geraniums?
What is there to love anymore, my friend?

Some days I, too, don't feel like going out.
Secluded with my gramophone
I play "Flores purisimas," zarzuela,
Caruso—over and over.

Once, years ago, I got lost in the vast cemetery of Milan.
I had my dog; I was taking roses to Toscanini's tomb.
It was an ordinary day,
Men were digging graves.

Confounded in the ballyhoo *Italien*,
The tombs carved like sailing ships,
I talked to perfect strangers:
Women alone with grief,
Men walking "on doctor's orders."

It is good, Borges, to have a mission, don't you agree?

Letter to Borges from Estonia

Where I go is of considerable doubt.
Winter, Tallinn, I climb aboard the wrong trolley.
Always a singular beam of light leads me astray.

After thousands of cities I am safe when I say, "It is always the wrong
       trolley"—
Didn't I love you with my whole heart? Athens? Dublin?

Solo gravitational effects: my body is light as a child's beside the botanical
       garden's iron fence—
But turning a corner one feels very old in the shadow of the
       mariners' church.

I ask strangers to tell me where I am.
Their voices are lovely, young and old.

Yes, I loved you with my whole heart.
I never had a map.

Coordinated, Platonic movement in deep snow.
Crooked doors and radios in the bread shops.

Letter to Borges from Galway

I go out in the early morning rain
And tap the cobblestones with my stick.
On my left, there is a river.
On my right, a loose window
Makes funereal percussions.
"Songs of Earth," I think.

I am not unique.
I stand beneath the shutter and weep.
I love this world.
I am alone in a new city.
If I died here beside the river and the window,
Maybe everything I've known
        would make sense in the gray of an Irish minute.

"Goodbye to the peregrine falcons," I think.
Goodbye to the glass of water that contains a single daylily.
Farewell to Mahler on the radio late at night.
Don't get me wrong:
I get lost in cities every week.

I have learned much by following the whims of architects.

Letter to Borges from London

When I was a boy I made a beehive
From old letters—dark scraps from a trunk,
Lost loves; assurances from travelers.
It was intricate work.
The blind kid and the worker bee lost whole days.
I made a library for inchworms.

Now I'm a natural philosopher but with the same restless hands.
Some days I put cities together—
Santiago and Carthage;
Toronto and Damascus.
If strangers watch closely, Borges,
They'll see my fingers working at nothing.

In Hyde Park near the Albert Memorial and alone on a bench
I reconstructed the boroughs of New York—
Brooklyn was at the center, Kyoto in place of Queens.
This was a city of bells and gardens, a town for immigrants.
The old woman passing by saw my hands at work.
She thought I was a lost blind man, a simpleton,
Said, "Poor Dearie!" and gave me a quid.

Why Poetry Surpasses Your Friends

for my stepson, Ross Connell, at sixteen

This is a poem with a gut ache and a broken lamp.
It used to be a hole; it used to be a burst tire.

Just so, you're the only one in the world.
You catch the insects of thought—

All the white-legged annihilations.
The poem knows. Says: *I am gall, I am heartburn. God's most
      deep decree.*
Bitter would have me taste: my taste was me.

Friends?
A bitter mystery?

It is good some days to keep quiet.
Our friends are disheveled wandering stars.

2

Do not smile at the simple myth, not even at the shallow one
for at the blackest sea it may be yours

GUNNAR EKELÖF (TRANSLATED BY
LEONARD NATHAN AND JAMES LARSON)

Early Conditions

I woke to rain.
And woke to houses in rain, children in rain.
And the morning news was wet withal, the news was drenched.
I wanted to prolong my waking, slow it, bank it like a fire,
Think. Hold dread. Stay still.
But the rain would have none of me.

That rain took the day for its own.
That rain had Aristotle
And algebra in every drop.
It had the spill of logic and the riff and roll of zero after zero.
It said it would not have me but that was all talk.
The rain the rain the rain the rain.

Letter from Vienna, Close of Day

Borges, you were in love with Kipling
And so I hear you in minutes
That can happen anywhere—poems of battle and imperial persuasion
Come over me—here in a peaceful city.
The anapests jangle,
The empire greases its bullets.

I expect little from the past. I walk about
Hearing the songs of thrushes—honestly—
And pause a moment.
Everything is just as it will.
Poplars sway.
Ravens turn their heads
And stare far off where the sun is also staring.

At the Winter Solstice, Iowa City

I listen for the footsteps
Of my dogs:

Little taps from their *via sacra*.
When I hear them on the stairs

I know the happiness
Of Vivaldi!

Borges, if only they'd given you a dog
You'd have known

Blindness stands for nothing.
—*Do not concern yourself with the whole.*

Alone

Today I understood
While drinking tea
And hearing rain
That the word for birth
And the one for sin
Come from a single sound
In Finnish—that tongue they
Spoke when I was small.
Synnty, untranslatable,
Original sin nearly,
But softer,
Like water
Carried a long way
In a jar
In May.

If You Ask

after the Finnish of Risto Rasa

My favorite walk
Was with a certain girl; we went along roads
Searching out preferred wildflowers
And going to and fro
Like that
Was a shared silence.
I suppose it's hard to have this nowadays.
And there were many horses watching
As we slipped through the wet grass,
And some flowers sparkled like match heads.
We went home with new ideas.
It was like wearing eyeglasses;
It was like sleeping
Inside a window.

Life in Wartime

There are bodies that stay home and keep living.
Wisteria and Queen Anne's lace
But women and children, too.
And countless men at gasoline stations.
Schoolteachers who resemble candles,
Boys with metabolisms geared to the future,
Musicians trying for moon effects.
The sky, which cannot expire, readies itself with clouds
Or a perfect blue
Or halos or the amoebic shapes
Of things to come.
The railway weeds are filled with water.
How do living things carry particles
Of sacrifice? Why are gods talking in the corn?
Enough to feel the future underfoot.
Someone is crying three houses down.
Many are gone or are going.

Prose Poem Written at 2 a.m.

I have decided to write while lying in bed.

Mark Twain used to do this though he did it by day and I'm doing it in the middle of the night while my wife is sleeping on her side of the bed.

As near as I can tell the chief merit of writing while lying flat on one's back in the dark is that you get to imagine you're a half-dead Englishman who has awakened in his tomb in London's Highgate Cemetery — and you're pulling on the rope that rings the bell outside so that presumably a man who is cutting the grass will hear your alarm and come running.

I once visited the tomb of Samuel Taylor Coleridge and sure enough there was a bell on the roof.

I saw six ravens standing beside Coleridge's bell.

They were congregating with the same easy indifference you see in street cops.

They were there out of habit.

And I pictured Coleridge in that sealed barrel vault pulling the cord with only the ravens within earshot.

I could see why the ravens liked their perch.

The tomb was atop a gentle hill and they could look out in all directions.

The first time I read Coleridge's poetry I was nineteen and I thought that being influenced in imaginative terms by an approaching storm was exciting.

Now I see that the storm never ends and that his old poem offers a false triangulation of rising and falling action.

Say what you will: bad weather and successive ravens are an unbroken and co-determinant chain and saying so won't make you feel any better.

I know that my will influences nothing in nature. The only thing I can cause by thinking is the accumulation of dust. I am good at this.

I have just now asserted that dust isn't a natural fact and that's foolish.

Poetry carves a topiary garden out of dust.

In a short while I shall abandon this business of writing in the dark and I'll switch on the radio and listen to the BBC and hear more about my country's foreign policy, which as far as I understand it is simply to kill as many civilians as we can. We kill them by arming their neighbors and by more direct means.

My country's chief exports are tears and dust.

"What about blood?" you ask. "Surely that's one of America's chief exports?"

Okay. Blood.

Please understand: I'm flat on my back in the middle of the night and I'm pulling the cord for all it's worth.

Of ravens I have not heard tell of any save that I know they are standing perfectly still on my roof and yours.

Now is the time of night for recalling past journeys.

In Lapland once I peered through a bus window with my blunted eyes and saw sparks imposed on the glass.

I thought of evening prayers in Khartoum and the silence of communal life after the day has gone.

I saw them, old men, long in their friendship, smoking as night filled their alley.

And there in my dark bus I imagined that one man had a child's toy: a wooden top that was likely a gift for his granddaughter. He set it spinning. It moved over the worn stones giving off a light that no one could explain.

It seems I am less of memory, more of dream. That's how it is after fifty.

I remember (inexactly) a boat ride with other children, summer in Finland, long ago.

There was a sickly boy seated at the bow.

An adult whispered the word *leukemia* but none of the children knew what that was.

It was the solstice, there was sun on water, a song about strawberries was going around.

Oh yes. I'm flat on my back and pulling this cord for all it's worth.

Letter from Saratoga, California

All day it rains
And I sit in a poplar—
Just another bird,

And owing to appetite
I don't know
How I got here.

I don't recall my homeland.
I don't know why, Borges,
But I think of a viola

Paganini
Kept in a glass case
And seldom played:

The beauty of its sound
Made him weep
Beyond measure.

Once I wrote in a journal,
When I couldn't tell how to live,
Lines about *Middlemarch:*

The way Eliot expresses doubt,
Dorothea doesn't whisper
But speaks boldly,

Steps to the curtain
Where the impossible light
Admits effects of loss—

Sun through the choked branches
Of Casaubon's wild garden.

Does need give us cunning, Borges?
Might we track one cycle of the rain
Like jazzmen,

That is,
Tempo fast
And vamping,

Storm rubato,
Storm
Old standard tune?

Can we play the jazz of blindness?
The unknown rhythm?
Absentminded

I listen to water.
It is a long way to morning.
Who serves jazz shall survive.

Approaching Rain

I live with the algebra of tears
Like anyone, pressing my face
To the lake, eyes opened.
Foolish, clumsy.

Look at him, old Aristotle
Bending to the marsh!
A man ill-formed with notions
Of gods or souls.

How sweetly he drinks
From what he doesn't understand.

But Seconds, Minutes of Life

after the Finnish of Risto Rasa

I watch from a bench
As crows wheel and land
Beside a sleeping dog:

The dog, so old,
Looks up
And the crows fly.

Dogs know a musical sadness when they wake.
Just as we do.

Book Review

after the Finnish of Pentti Saarikoski, who
wrote of reading Gyula Illyés in the sauna

I want you to buy this
Because when I take it in the sauna
It sweats like an old man,
One who has lived in exile
From his country,
One who recalls hymns
When the weather is good,
Who sings bawdy songs
When it rains in winter—
Old book of anarchist's prose,
Quick for the eyeing, but not too quick,
It leaves you cold though you're laughing,
Though you're sweating through this life,
Green with notions, starved with God,
Inconsolable with every page.

Normal

The King of Sweden is normal:
Newspapers say so,
And the woman
Selling flowers
Says so
From her kiosk
Outside
The station.
She displays
His photograph
Above
Azaleas.

And children
Agree,
Even
The little ones
With bulky
Snowsuits
And faces
Pinched
As old philosophers;
They know
The king
Is normal,
He has
Buttons
All down
His front.

The trolley driver
Who must pass
A funeral home
Each morning
Knows
The king
Is normal;
He is there,
Painted
On plate glass,
Grieving
For the nation,
He is
A good king
Sober
And dressed
Like a judge.

When women gather
In the church
To sew
Tiny flags
In remembrance
Of the dead
They
See the king's picture
On the packages
Of needles.

He sees far,
This king;
This king
Attends
The circus
And sits high up;
He is
Never too old;
Some claim
To have seen him
As an infant
Or later
Walking with a stick,
But they
Are surely mad.

Café Solo with an Old Horn

after the Finnish of Turkka Suominen

COLUMBUS. What were you thinking?
       I was the one who found India.
ODYSSEUS. I'm the only one who got home.

◄

Heaven is crowded
With rudely built houses
But the machines are white,
Things go smoothly.
Of course one can see stars
Shining beneath the streets.
I won't get to heaven,
Probably won't see those stars.
I'm working the rounds
With this broom.
I did see constellations
Above your head
Before you disappeared.

◄

When you light my cigarette
Just that way,
I am smoke.

Apple Mazurka

One dances this with a spoon and the crack
Of an arthritic knee—dancing for once

Without plans. No one needs to know.
Without plans you dance clear out

Of the cemetery road, of first names
And last, villages, old streets, old houses.

Come trumpet, Turkish drum,
We dance for the neighbor's dead—

Dance, hell, for pepper and wheat.
Give it away like a good dance.

Dance it up under birches
Where the crown longs to return.

By Halves

Mind by halves thinks "ethics"—
Erases ethics, writes "only."

My uncle washed with gin
Thought "defensible" since

He was cross, he was tired.
He lost the book of ethics.

By halves we are ready.
By halves men storm a beach.

Don't we whisper in halves?
I strive to be half a man.

I ache for half the moon,
Half of love, half the luck song

Sung by the cricket
Who sings with half his leg.

Jazz from Cripple City

I saw tonight four men in wheelchairs eating
Flowers, laughing through the dusk
In a public garden.
Forsythia leaned to the water.
Oh, to bear up under such rollicking measures.
Oh, to live in Buffalo, New York, and eat civic plantings.

Yes, it's true:
A friend had to tell me about the men who ate from the soil.
Her description was full of detail, let us say, as
The courts are full of law,
As Doc Williams might have said.

But no one can describe the murmurous laughter that does not
Alter the case and the twilight full of sounds.

The War Production Canzone

Whirlpool: Imagine It
ADVERTISING SLOGAN

I have come at last
To understand
The power
Of my dishwasher:
I use it
To bring back
The dead!
Don't kid yourself,
The dead
Live on
In proximity
To machines
And why shouldn't
My dishwasher
Become
A Tibetan
Portal—
A Bardo-matic
Multicycle
Soul cleanser?
I set the dial
To Advanced Patriotism
Making sure
To add
The Orphic spot-remover,
And
Let the falling
Inertia
Of the unreal dead
Wash backward

42

Into history
With the fused stones
And magic gems
Of unfathomable
Becoming.
And how quietly
My dishwasher
Shifts
Into
The Pythagorean
Cycle!

The mathematic
Flesh and bone
Stirs
With
Leaf pattern,
Scarlet berries,
Until
My good
Dishwasher,
My Whirlpool
From RCA,
A corporation
Heavily invested
In weapons
Of mass destruction
Lo!
My death-ray
Dishwasher

Raises up
Out of the mineral earth
Those
Who once
Were buyer
And seller,
Master
And victim,
Foot soldiers,
Iraqi children,
Kurds,
Sandinistas,
Contras,
Maoists,
Integrationists,
Trotskyites,
Mensheviks,
You get the picture
And
My dishwasher
Makes a sound
Like wings
And washes out
All the *blood-drenched*
Civilized
Abstractions
Of the rascals
Who live
By killing
You and me.

BUSINESS REPLY MAIL
FIRST-CLASS MAIL   PERMIT NO. 43   PORT TOWNSEND WA

POSTAGE WILL BE PAID BY ADDRESSEE

Copper Canyon Press
PO Box 271
Port Townsend, WA 98368-9931

NO POSTAGE
NECESSARY
IF MAILED
IN THE
UNITED STATES

So, what do you think?

Book Title:

Comments:

Can we quote you on that? ☐ yes ☐ no

Copper Canyon Press seeks to build the awareness of, appreciation of, and audience for a wide range of emerging and established American poets, as well as poetry in translation from many of the world's cultures, classical and contemporary. To receive our catalog, send us this postage-paid card or email your contact information to poetry@coppercanyonpress.org

NAME:

ADDRESS:

CITY:

STATE: ZIP:

EMAIL:

☐ Send me *Editor's Choice*, a bimonthly email of poems from forthcoming titles.

COPPER
CANYON
PRESS

www.coppercanyonpress.org

3

Mist suddenly appears at midocean.... No assurances in the ocean.

ROBERT BLY

Letter to Borges from North Carolina

You were right:
Reality is not always probable, or likely.
A policeman said I was jaywalking
And I had to tell him
I couldn't see.
(I'd been all day
In a library
Where Doubt
And a Minotaur
Entertained themselves
And then
I was walking beside them
In the Carolina dusk.)

How do you talk to a cop?
I felt like a god
Descending.
I was a Minoan "master of animals"
Consecrated
To red and green,
The underworld colors of first sight.

How do you tell strangers
That people may live
Who cannot see?
Not easy—
Harder than books.

A house in blindness.
Blindness
A house
Of observances
And nothing more than empty air.

Letter to Borges from Tampere, Finland

Winnowing and threshing in the far north—
Sunlight like tea in a glass (a stranger
Tells me) and local musicians play waltzes
In a coffee bar. Borges,
I got a bit drunk last night
And walked into a field and lay down where
The Caterpillar machines had torn a long seam in the earth
And the waltzing was, as the Finns say, *nurin kurin,* all topsy-turvy
In my head,
And my ruined eyes took the roses and broken shards
Of twilight and built another village—a countervillage
Where the houses stood like wineglass stems.
You could see through everything—
Even the walls of the church—
A fact that didn't bother anyone,
As men and women made of light
Are necessarily long-lived and unconcerned
About the hour.

49

Letter to Borges from Madrid

It was early
And in the café
Whores dropped ice in their beer.
I played chess in the mega-etheric garden—
You know,
A place like the rim between sea and sky.

I wanted to call my father, long dead,
Tell him the mind is a fit tribute to the world.
The whores knew as much, fingered their matches and found objects:
Combs, finger rings, spectacles, reminder notes from strangers.
Even where there isn't much light we live eye to eye.
It's a shame really, there was no one to call.

Letter to Borges from Helsinki

I will never get tired of this city that's blue as a shinbone, blue as a pair of false teeth, blue as the eyes of a fish, blue as my grandfather's schoolbook. And the children sleep in their prams, bundled against the cold, thin little vapors like smoky needles rising from their unformed faces—one sees them on every street, small, seemingly abandoned bundles devoting themselves to the subconscious. No sign of their parents: it's a matter of common sense to put your baby out alone in the winter. City as blue as your dead mother's curtains, blue as an old soldier's wrist, blue and blue and blue and blue and blue and blue.

Letter to Borges from Los Angeles

Mockingbirds everyplace,
Mary Pickford, all the gamines
Call
From on high—

    Dare to be foolish,
Study the role.

      Silly to think
Homilies of Ælfric
While hauling
A bag
Of oranges
Up
Rodeo—

Also to dead
Good message was told,

And think of Christ
Stirring the inferno,
The good odor of his news
Waking spirits.

Borges,
Hell took a body
And found God—

Lovely birds
Put this in mind
In a town
Not my own.

Letter to Borges from Graz

I spent last night drinking with two madmen.

We sat up late in a summer garden and laughed like mad about the mercenary bullshit of capitalism.

One of us played the accordion.

One of us had actually been to Tuva.

Otto said the throat singers are enormously fond of marijuana.

Otto and I talked about the business of traveling when a man is blind.

"You wake up somewhere, facedown in fragrant leaves, and you don't know if you've been captured, or perhaps you have, against all odds, arrived in heaven," he said.

Letter to Borges from Dublin

The moon swims back and forth with insolence no matter whether Ireland
      is rich or poor.
Entire lives turn over: the old are young once again,
The young break clean in the currents of stars.

Borges, the moon combs dark paving stones—
It follows the lines of streets.
The light it casts is a poor man's fence.

Can I say my faith is stirred?
This light proclaims there is justice,
And I can still make it out with these ruined eyes.

Letter to Borges from Houston, Texas

I fell down this morning, Borges. I blamed this on the pavement outside
the hotel.
There is something about falling when you're blind, a kind of synesthesia
occurs,

I fell slowly into a cold paradise of blue.
It was like falling into the world in the birth wind.

Do you remember that?

Falling like this is certainly a kind of nostalgia.
I had time to think.

"Only God can conceal God,"
That's what I thought.

My arms were extended like wings.
Joyfully, falling.

I should add that no one was awake to see me.
Borges, did you ever laugh in so much blue?

Letter to Borges from Grazer Schloßberg

Tourists are fighting at a nearby table
In this café close to the mountain,
Something about losing their map or the tickets.
My French isn't what it used to be.

Borges, I recall your witty comment on the Falklands War,
Britain and Argentina:
"Two bald men fighting over a comb."
It was worse than that of course:
Thousands dead for an ink stain.

Still, I like the morning
Taking the lottery of streets as they come.

No one should confuse aestheticism with sightlessness
Or blindness with desire.

In general, meeting people
Is the antidote
To airs of dissolution.

I am trying to learn patience through tenderness.

London, Summer Heat Wave

I exited the tube at Paddington station.
London is the only city in the world where the drunks make noise when
       it's hot.

Borges, I thought of Kipling; thought of your own taut meters.
But not all blind men seek order.

Purgatorial drinkers in a local pub shouted at German footballers on TV
And why not? And a woman was dancing on the bar and why not?

The world was topsy-turvy and it was short on seriousness and why not?

You couldn't find an Apollonian man for miles.

Letter to Borges from New York City

You can get lost between heartbeats and strangers will know.

I climbed out of a carriage at Central Park and I heard a man speaking
    Russian to his horse.

I was lost just then and believed the cabman's horse
Knew full well my predicament.

I suspected the horse was staring into the late autumn sun.

I heard two men arguing about how to carry a sheet of glass when the
    wind is fierce.

We are never far from the circus or the general belief in alchemy.

On Fifth Avenue, Paracelsus still makes his living selling thimbles and
    miniature Greek flags.

Letter to Borges from Pittsburgh

Hotel radio. Bessie Smith. Clouds knocking at the window by God.

Outside a Sunday silence, old Carnegie having his way—even the wheels must be quiet.

A friend tells me my writing is too "experiential" but I can't afford to let it bother me: The forests of blindness are like the daydreams of the robber barons, you move the buildings and streets in your head, build a vast dynamo throwing sparks along the Ohio River. Eventually you imagine that the world looks like the paradisial village square that one sees upon waking. Sparks over the dark water.

Nowadays Pittsburgh is clean.

There are good people here.

When I walk in the early morning I feel alone in the unquiet way known to all guilty men.

I want to send an old-fashioned telegram:

Western wind stop Police place straw in the streets to muffle the sounds of carriages per Andrew Carnegie's orders.

Letter to Borges from Porvoo, Finland

This is a town of antique wooden houses.

My wife has entered a shop that sells, what else? miniature wooden houses.

I sit under an oak tree with my loyal guide dog who is scenting the April wind with her leonine face.

Wooden houses. Wooden houses. *Hauskaa Joulua,* Merry Christmas, carve us a house, old man, won't you?

The young men sit up at night, drinking and smoking until dawn. They don't mean to do it, but they invariably set fire to their innocent houses. They tell jokes and fall asleep.

Helsinki burned down some three hundred years ago. Back in those days the city was built entirely of wood.

The capital was even then a young man's town.

Porvoo's houses have survived because all the men traveled far into the world.

And the wooden houses still wait like beached ships.

It's April. Clear and dry. The Finnish winter is over at last.

Borges, you can sit outside in Porvoo and you won't hear a sound.

Letter to Borges from Turku, Finland

Borges, I walked a generous and slow compass around the old church:

A fishermen's church, built with narrow windows.

I was lonesome all day, walking alone in the far north,

Gulls danced sideways at my feet,

My white cane tapped the cobblestones.

It was summer but you wouldn't know it.

I walked my circle.

Old women sold lingonberries to laughing children.

A dog was barking at Swedish ghosts.

Years ago, twenty, precisely,

I phoned the Finnish poet Saarikoski.

He was in Sweden,

Reagan was planning to nuke the East—

I called the dying poet

To talk about minotaurs.

Snakes underfoot. Crows in a cage.

The Boolean algebra of Palestrina.

Heraclitus and Greek vowels.

James Joyce

And the hot, little abacus

Of syllabic Finno-Ugrian jazz.

Saarikoski got on the line.

"Maybe we will meet one day in this mad world," he said.

Today I traced a clean circle with my feet

Though I didn't see the city in which I walked.

I thought of the candles in Turku's church, candles cold as glass, even
    in summer.

Why this consistent sadness, Borges?

I am in Madrid where there's singing in the streets.
Did this ever happen to you? The meeting breaks up
And the people lock eyes and talk
As if they were always friends.
How lonesome I feel just then.
I'm like a man alone on a raft.
Madrid is hot today. The Plaza Mayor
Crackles with circus music
As if the people were going together
To a scene of resurrection.
I'm at the back of the crowd
Talking to myself, as usual;
I smell the perfume
As the many rush past me.
What a qualified loneliness this is, Borges!
I think it is a smuggler's art,
Walking outside of time where ordinary coins are useless.

Without Stars

We might say, as Auden did, the stars are all indifferent.
But now, past fifty I don't know, the conceit may turn
From a life of cheer as the poet had good drink

And those who loved him; we may call the stars unfriendly
When we are snug at home, the fire banked,
Our paschal lamb with pepper, the wine dark.

We might say we are more loving and be true
As love is to sky—a small advantage
And love-me-not is the name of its tune

Which stars cannot know.
Here's a succession of rooms,
Dresses and trousers, our heaped books;

The ailanthus we hope to plant come May—
In the garden we'll be powerless,
Ailanthus cannot grow

Until the leaves are strong
And we would
Be more loving

If we but knew the words.
Still, I will call the stars unfriendly
Only when I'm far from home.

Borges: They Are Knocking the Wind out of Me in Iowa City

Up late, reading alone I saw how Minturno was fooled by the intricacies of beauty. Unfortunately at that hour there was no one to tell. As a friend once wrote: "Everyone I know is either dead or still asleep."

"Don't talk to yourself," I told myself. "Don't scribble in the margins."

When Marsilio Ficino said that beauty was just shapes and sounds, he was surely bathing outdoors.

Neoplatonists ease their bodies into their warm baths. Close your eyes you can see Minturno bathing under the autumn stars.

And so I went to bed at last and dreamt of my first city—Helsinki, late fifties—the old man in the harbor selling potatoes from a dory. In the dream, as in life, that old man was wearing a red shirt, the first I ever saw.

Minturno: ideal forms are the source of our passionate failures.

The next morning I walked in the street and felt too many things to be judged a success.

A man on stilts was handing out flyers announcing the arrival of a circus. It was a French circus. The man was speaking French.

"Ah," he said in French, "you are blind."

He withdrew the flyer and tottered away.

66

I resisted the impulse to shout after him in my high-school French: "You sound like the first dull minute after a train wreck!"

The stilts made a metallic ticktock on the paving stones.

"Ticktock, train wreck," I said to myself, feeling my tongue dent the soft palate. That was my method of keeping silent. Ticktock.

Letter to Borges from Troy, New York

Borges, once there was a shirt factory
But grass hides the spot.

Garment workers stood above stamping machines.

When I was ten
I found a book
Of Egyptian love poems
At a pawnshop
Where now the street
Is broken
Into particulate and civic news.

4

A mild wind goes through the landscape.

I mean, our complaining must also come to an end.

LARS GUSTAFSSON (TRANSLATED BY
YVONNE L. SANDSTROEM)

As for the World

in memory of Deborah Tall

You who loved the bitter seeds in bread and poems.
You who never saw devils.
You who laughed at the felicities
Of Russian rhymes.

Winter wheat showed today, its infused green.
A red-tailed hawk I've come to know
Stayed all morning in his oak.
Goodbye. Goodbye.
The rhymes remain.

Sundays in Ohio

Bread turns stale in a paper sack.
The word *Jerusalem* sleeps
On children's tongues.
In the last days of school I wake them
And help them with their books.

A bowl of oranges
Warms in the sun, the fruit
Fattens. Coffee steams.
Pages of algebra
Lie everywhere.

One still finds on Sundays
Houses at auction, the old people
Gone in the tailored light
Beyond pin oaks
And photos of newlyweds
Holding the unselfish flowers of summers
And behind them grass and space.

The Iowa River

I followed the river and of course
The river followed me.

We didn't have permission,
We didn't make ourselves large.

The river said it was newly blind.
I was newly blind —

Willows at a bend
Filled with crows.

"We happen," I thought,
"Where pinweed

Spreads its light."
All thinking rivers

Stay quiet — or not —
Roots tangle,

Current flows.
I pressed my face

Against the river
And the river

Alighted
Anywhere it pleased.

Lullaby: Happenstance Blues

Heaven gives us pause, forgive me—
Don't want to step on your toes;

There's no soft gold.
There's no gold at all.

I wanted to be a good child once,
Thought I'd be king of the moon

And now I believe in nothing
But my own quiet room.

Kansas: Deaf Girl Watching the Moon

for Brenda Brueggemann

One night there are valleys,
Say around eleven,
When the moon is wide
As a brother's grin.
The field is black as shadow:
Soybeans sleep in loops
Of darkness,
Their leaves curled.
The valleys of the moon,
As unalike as pitted stones
Or walls or men
Or water or dreams—
Unalike as pages in a book.
When he saw them,
The valleys like hands,
Valleys like the bones of hands,
Galileo rushed into the street
Hoping for someone to tell.
He had no field.
He could not talk with his hands.

Elegy for Ray Charles and His Mother

Ray, no one knows what it's like to carry water
The way your mother made you carry it—

Even the boy Pharaoh
Wore a yoke on his shoulders

Just to show he was a man.
History doesn't matter much,

At least until your child
"Done gone blind"—your mama saw it—

"You always got to carry water," she said.
"This ain't no kidding around."

Long time
You carried water

In both hands,
Feeling for the path

With your feet.
Ray, your mama knew—

A song comes that way—
Or else it never will.

Laugh or cry it's the same.
A mockingbird listens from a telephone wire.

Long time, water, both hands.

Elegy for Lucy Grealy

Lucy, I put your planet on the table
And sectioned it like fruit.
I felt wise, avant-garde—
Making a place to love
Is about taking love apart,
Not about assembly.
And the planet on the table
Always behaved, never struggled.
It knew its role, came apart
Like the moon in Spain:
That moon of coins
That broke for Goya.

Every crippled kid grows up
To play at doctor:
Cut the patient,
Bury him with dimes and string.
The summer I met you
The victory swallows
Talked like mad.
You gave me your poems.
I saw horses, flight,
A meadow, some dancing.
And I took your poems apart,
Closing, twisting your lines.

I hadn't read your book,
Was too blind
To see your face.

I saw you write me off—
Why not? There were boys
At MacDowell—
You bragged
About screwing one
On a pool table
And I went on cutting
The blue planet.
I thought about lines
I could cut
From every book on Earth.

And very late, a thin wash
Of cirrus clouds
Crossed the fields.
I walked my dog
By the three-quarter moon.
And heard you then, far ahead,
Laughing with a man,
And everywhere
There was the smell
Of cinnamon ferns and hay.

Autobiographia Literaria

Johnny Nolan has a patch on his ass
Kids chase him
LAWRENCE FERLINGHETTI

Oh, I had that thing—
Patch on the ass,
Gauzy SOS dangling
Like a fig,
Stain on the world—
        And the kids who ate dirt,
Geniuses all—
They knew
The sign—
        Bull's-eye;
Local flag;
Dog in the manger;
Birthmark;
        Patch on the ass;
And God have mercy—
Running for your life
Hoping
Just that once
To *cut out*
Into stray eternity;
Morse code in your head;
        Patch on the ass;
        Patch on the ass;
And streetlights coming on.

For Anyone at All

After the clock was done with noon
The boy leapt up like a crow
To land in the great dictionary.

Like an ape he tore the pages,
Applied some paste with a stick
Until he held a doll of sorts,

A puppet made of words.
He could hear the neighbor's
Children at a window: *Hey*

Blind boy—find us where we are!
Come on and guess!
He waved the pages then,

Making them bow and rise
Like nothing you will ever see.

Dream in D Minor

for my wife, Connie Kuusisto

I woke in the night
To your steady breathing,
Checked the clock
As rain tapped the window.

The throaty voice
Of your sleep
Sang of long shores
And a girlhood

Of horses,
A noon path
In snow, spruces,
A bridle

Flashing
And cold sun
Lighting
The silver hills

And the horses,
I thought,
Preening the way they do
With their great eyes.

I saw them, the horses,
Standing under trees
Dark and alone
With you.

Poems in a Book

after the Finnish of Jarkko Laine

Words written
As night comes,
A green ribbon of dusk,
Blossoms in the apple trees
And the wind just so.

The grass stays warm; faces of the stones stay warm
So that joy doesn't disappear
All at once.
Wind half of sorrow now.

Today I was alone
Reading by a creek,
Tracking bits of philosophy
Much as a schoolboy
Watches hornets
In the still of afternoon.

Sometimes, end of day, the poem
Follows me—
And unmindful,
Or
As if I alone
Could have my say,
I go on arguing
With houses and barns,
Dream structures
Of the solstice.

Autumn Comedy

after the Finnish of Risto Rasa

I was cloudy all day:
I had clouds in the bones.
There were clouds

In the tissues of my hands.
"This is not so hard," I thought.
"I can stand in the orchard

With no more hope
Than that old horse."
The clouds were fast!

And then I was chewing
A windfall apple
And planning my sainthood.

The Summer Chairs

This morning we carried
The summer chairs indoors
And put our boat in storage

As if in the city of the dead
There's a need for oars or sails.
Flowers, domestic—

Take them to the woods.
The birches
Spoke of new arrangements.

In the woodpile
Crickets sang
Long, dark praises.

Inside
We covered tables,
Put away the lamps.

At a window
We saw a wolf spider
Pinnacle her web

Bright as pins;
It was almost time to leave.
We looked around.

Everything was present.
The hermit thrush,
The water.

They Say

In Korea they say
The crow has twelve
Notes, none of them
Music—not surely.
And here, early,
A pine thrush
Sang when it felt
Hunger, invited
Nowhere—its
Music came down
Heavily on desire.

In substance
I side with the crow
Whose sound
Is borne heavily—
Because the notes
Are not music,
Because the crow's
Satori
Is a mistake,
Singing that way
To pure, endless joy.

Hornets in a Woodpile

I like them because they come from a dead star,
Because they are purposeful and mindless.

The electrolysis of summer air
Is in their wings and pinched waists.

The labor of anger and of forgetting
Is in their cut eyes.

They float among stacked pine boards
Until they appear tireless:

Gravity cannot stop them, the hours
Will pass them over.

They lift slowly in the shadows,
Move through the woodpile without god.

"If a Nightingale Could Sing like You"

for David Weiss

Watching the Marx Brothers in Ashtabula
Is, of course, the title of a poem yet to be
Written. I love
An earlier scene in the film where Harpo
And Chico, disguised as barbers, destroy
The captain's mustache while feigning
Concern for aesthetics. It's the first fully
Postmodern movie ever made. Stowaways
In the bilge of capitalism. Each of them
Driven second by second by hormones
And appetites and every moment Harpo
forgetting what he's doing because he
Sees a Bryn Mawr coed in a tennis outfit.
Every authority figure is a fraud. Dirty
Money and guns everywhere. Thorstein
Veblen gagged and bound in the Purser's
Office. And the funniest joke of all—
They have to sneak into France. No
One sneaks into France. Only the pure
Of heart would have trouble getting in.
Only the pure of heart would pretend
To be Maurice Chevalier and disguise
Themselves solely by singing his songs.
The jokes are all so elegant and
They are always stealing dinner rolls.
Once I was in Ashtabula, did I ever tell
You that, where the lake is Erie. What
Else but Harpo batting his eyes
Could make the ashes on our plate

Palatable? So, here's to Pig Alley
And to the girl (Lillian Gish) who rejects
Snapper Kid but lies to protect him from
The police. Sometimes that's all you get.

Ode to Victor Frankenstein

for Donald Rumsfeld

You did it: you made a brother, a father.
You made a kind of mule—
A poor man's mule
With discolored eyes.
You built him so he would follow;
You made him lonely;
Gave him you;
Perfect in the giving:
No language;
Forests of veins;
Knees and ears; art
Of lost walking.

And when you ran
You gave him division;
So even his new life
Was old.

The Lottery Sellers

They will be gone by now, the blind lottery sellers of Athens, swept from the streets in time for the Olympics. Even the Greek businessmen sipping coffee in the streetside cafés find these old men selling paper tickets to be embarrassing, a reminder of the Middle Ages or worse: they are the blind of Sophocles, their voices twisted and keening. "Buy some luck," they cry, swaying under yokes of hanging tickets.

Everyone knows the age of luck is over. We have entered the age of muscle.
A waiter carries a Chilean sea bass to the table.
The lottery sellers will be taken to the country;
This won't be anything new. They will play chess. Some will play fiddles.
The time for luck will come around again.

Erasing Stars

A teacher of standing, a poet, tells her class, *Never put stars in your poems,* and some of the students write this down. And some stop writing after a year or two. And some get married or take jobs selling pharmaceuticals. And some think, *Time is in short supply,* and ex cathedra take up parent worship.

I know a Baltic poet who draws Egyptian star charts on cocktail napkins as he answers questions. I also know a poet in Tucson, an amateur ornithologist who believes that stars influence birds. "Of course," he says, "the carbon in our brains comes from stars."

Erase stars from a page. Nothing happens. The allotropic pulse of mathematics ticks anyway. But now try putting the stars back. It can't be done. This failure has nothing to do with personal habits.

History in Empty Air

1

When Rilke arrived in Paris he went straight to his room at 11 rue Toullier
And opened his accordion case and raised to a dirty window
A photograph of his mother. How beautiful she'd been!

In her twenties she was an olive tree; one of Hera's own,
And her hair was dark and luxuriant, held neatly by pins.
By a trick of light it became again wine-red and night-blue—

Her hair that had smelled of fire
That threatened always to come unbound
As she fixed the buttons of his bristling dress.

2

I believe he headed next to the street
To see in faces the workings of God,
Cliché and conviction,
A freshness in strangers,
Something that night would steal incrementally—
His glances had to be quick.
He walked in lugubrious circles around the hospital.
He practiced watching while tying his shoe.

3

In 1902 Paris was still a city of medieval streets—transverse,
Crowded with blind men, prostitutes, tubercular children.
"Here," he thought, "is what happens.

94

The evenhandedness of God is a gray thing.
It rolls and knocks us down. There is no time to prepare.
Often the victim doesn't die
But remains a long time in God's streets."

Rilke, with the eyes of an eternal wanderer.

4

A tailor wrote on dark wool with a wax pencil;
A funeral carpenter screwed a brass nameplate on a coffin's lid;
A baker marked yellow meringue with his finger;
The poet filled his pockets with irresolute names.

A very old woman fed honey-colored crusts to a dog.
He saw her as a life's work—thought of her soul burning—
She was so old, in essence, she had outstepped her body.
The dog swayed on its hip joints and lifted its face.
The woman reached, bread shaking,
While above them the bakery's awning stiffened in the wind.

Elegy for a Guide Dog

Corky, where you are now; can you see again?
Are you free of the aches and all the uncoiled walking
That we do down here—
We've forgotten something and must make our way
Down this lonesome street
On a summer's day.
Oh, my dear, no one can match your stride.
Are you in the tall grass
Informed perfectly by light?

Letter to Borges from Syracuse

Down where the great tenor must have felt it, under my left-side low rib
There was a green fruit, a pear of the mind, moonlit, cold and wet.

I felt it early, bending to the paper, just a curve
From the torso, a twist

That was not me, do you understand? I called to a bird
In the catalpa, called it bird-wise, soft

But to no effect. I was rich,
Alive, with nowhere to go, fruit from a dream

Hanging where my lungs and diaphragm met.
I wanted to stay there always,

Do you understand? My blindness was just a nuisance.
The pear, an unworldly thing,

Swayed, understand, and grew on nothing.

ABOUT THE AUTHOR

Stephen Kuusisto is a graduate of Hobart College and the Writers' Workshop at the University of Iowa. He has studied as a Fulbright Scholar in Finland and currently directs the Renée Crown University Honors Program at Syracuse University, where he holds a university professorship in the Center on Human Policy, Law, and Disability Studies. He speaks widely on literature, diversity, disability, education, and public policy. He is the author of *Eavesdropping: A Memoir of Blindness and Listening* and the acclaimed memoir *Planet of the Blind*, a New York Times Notable Book of the Year. His debut collection of poems, *Only Bread, Only Light,* was published in 2000 by Copper Canyon Press. Recognized by the *New York Times* as "a powerful writer with a musical ear for language and a gift for emotional candor," Kuusisto has made numerous appearances on National Public Radio and the BBC, and on programs such as *The Oprah Winfrey Show* and *Dateline NBC*. Visit his website at www.stephenkuusisto.com.